Fish by Candlelight

JIN Bo
Translated by
Huaicun Zhang
Wang Dan

Young Paths
青岛出版集团 | 青岛出版社

This book is the result of a co-publication agreement
between Qingdao Publishing House Co., Ltd.
(CHINA) and Paths International Ltd (UK)

Title: Fish by Candlelight
Author: Jin Bo
Translated by Zhang Huaicun, Wang Dan
Hardback ISBN: 978-1-84464-707-1
Paperback ISBN: 978-1-84464-708-8
Ebook ISBN: 978-1-84464-709-5
Copyright © 2023 by Young Paths Childrens Books LTD.

The copyright to this title is owned by Qingdao
Publishing House Co., Ltd. (CHINA) and Young Paths
Children Books LTD which is an imprint of Paths
International Ltd. U.K. This book is made available
internationally through an exclusive arrangement with
Paths International Ltd of the United Kingdom and is
permitted for sale worldwide.

青岛出版集团 | 青岛出版社

Young Paths Childrens Books LTD.
Paths International Ltd
www.pathsinternational.com
Published in United Kingdom

Fish by Candlelight

JIN Bo

Translated by
Huaicun Zhang
Wang Dan

青岛出版集团 | 青岛出版社

To seek for beauty, kindness and truth

—Preface of 'Children Counting for Stars'

In various literary styles, poetry has a natural connection with children. Children normally get closest to poetry as it inhabits their heart and is in the depth of their soul.

Children can learn poetry without a teacher because they have innocent feelings and rich imagination which are also the characteristics of poetry. Another characteristic is the musicality of poetry, the rhythm of which can directly reaching the soul and soothe it. Children can easily accept it through listening.

Children are born with innocence, imagination, and ability to listen to beautiful sounds. If children are given attention and enlightenment, they will know how to appreciate and listen to poetry.

We must work hard to take care of such poetic heart. When children are illiterate and unable to read the poems autonomously, they should be leaded into the "Poetry of Sound" that can be entered into their ears and rooted in their hearts. With the "Poetry of Sound" in mind, their hearing is comforted,

which is also an artistic enjoyment. Therefore, we can say that the aesthetic taste of babies starts with sound; specifically, it starts with reading poems (children's rhymes). The children's rhymes can coordinate movements, add interest to the game, or even make children fall asleep peacefully as a lullaby. "Poetry of sound" is the first lesson in the initial aesthetic enjoyment of life. The rhythm of poetry is naturally integrated with poetry. Poems without rhythms are difficult to remember or spread.

When children can read independently, they have more choices. They can read myths, fairy tales, adventure stories, and fables. However, reading poems is also important at this time. Children's spiritual state and language expression ability can be enhanced by delight, charm, philosophical thinking, and subtle language expression in poems. Cultivating the pure interest of literature also depends on reading and appreciating poems.

We often say that poetry is literature in literature. We also say that literature is the foundation of various arts. The value of poetry is clearly demonstrated by those comments. I once delivered," Reading poetry is not a general pastime, it can allow readers to get the joy and nourishment of reading from pure literary. The knowledge, such as emotions excited by music, feelings

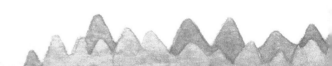

aroused by art painting, and enchantments from songs and dances, will make us understand the difference between reading poetry and reading other literary styles. "

We traditionally value poetic education which is always accompanied with emotions and deep-feelings.

Poetry offers us a keen eye to seek for beauty, that is, paying attention to life, nature and others. When finding beauty, our thoughts will be richer and our heart more abundant. Poetry also leads us continuously to explore the beautiful surroundings and to follow atmosphere in poetry with freshness and curiosity.

Poetry requests us to be kind. Reading poetry means communicating with the world, with the others, and with oneself, that is, perceiving harmony and sincerity, gasping gentleness and honesty, and understanding dignity and prestige. Excellent poems are a guide to kindness.

Poetry increases us the wisdom for truth. We will be touched and start to meditate by reading poetry, and consequently have not only aesthetic taste but also power of critical thinking. Some poems are beautiful and creative, and some are sensible and vigorous. However, those particularly used as aphorisms, can even enlighten the mind and encourage people to pursue the truth.

In short, we will feel peaceful from reading poetry, understand life, enjoy

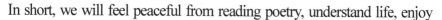

life and encourage ourselves to build up a better life. We will also achieve triumph from reading poetry, gaining rich imagination that is even more powerful than the knowledge. People will be smarter, more sensible, and more ingenious in childhood if he is fond of poetry.

This set of poems in front of you is a well-crafted display of current children's poetry in China which contains all the characteristics of poetry I mentioned above, combining with beautiful words, fantastic pictures and lovely sounds.

I hope that all of you enjoy these poems.

Jin Bo
7th April 2017

Contents

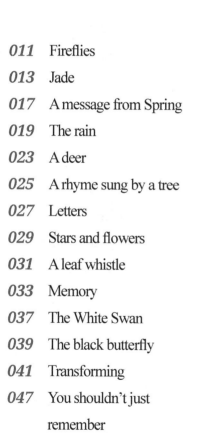

Fireflies

I will not tailor the splendid sunset for you.
Nor will I pick up the stars twinkling at night.
My dear, let's go together
To catch the fireflies dancing in the twilight.

The clouds turn into purple,
Slowly integrating into dusk.
The glorious flowers disappear.
The mountain only shows a tall shadow.

Look, there comes a few fireflies,
With a flickering light,
Like a star, two stars,
And millions of stars with wings.

I pull out a scallion from the vegetable garden
To put the fireflies into its long stalk.
With a soft light flashing in,
Here it is, my dear, a greenish lamp for you.

Put the lamp by your pillow,
I then create a fairy tale:
Once upon a summer night,
There was an emerald dream...

Written in 1979

Jade

My daughter Jade and I,
We come to look for you,
Green, the beautiful colour green,
Where are you?

In early spring, mountains are in the distance,
On the body of which trees are growing.
The beautiful colour green is covering,
As dense as a fog.

We come to look for you,
Green, the beautiful colour green.
But in the mountains or woods,
We cannot find you.

After breezing for a while,
And raining throughout the night,
The sun finally comes out.
All of a sudden, we see you.

(Were you coming with the wind
hiding in the rain,
Or casted down by the sun?
Please answer me, Green, the beautiful colour green.)

Mountains are in the distance,
dressing in green.
On their body, trees are growing,
Who turn into green, the beautiful green.

In the twigs of saplings
Green brooks are running
Into a pool of water,
Where a duck can dye its wings green.

Dews are gleaming on the grass,
As green as emeralds.
Birds are singing in the morning,
A song of green.

Look at my daughter Jade,
Whilst she is looking for you,
You are reflecting on her plaits
As well as in her bright eyes.

Here comes the spring,
Whom we wish to stay forever.
My dear daughter Jade, now you should know
Why you have such a name.

Written in 1980

A message from Spring

The wind decorates tree branches in green.

The water paints duck feathers in white.

After waiting for a whole winter,

Here arrives Spring.

Put on our spring clothes,

Just like birds replacing feathers.

When they are flying through the woods and over the hills,

The giggling of Spring can be heard all over the world.

I see the first butterfly dancing,
Who leads me to wherever it passes.
I happily catch it,
And let it go thereafter.

I see the first daisy blooming,
Who makes me keep jumping for joy.
Dear little daisy, do you still remember me?

When coming to the branches where leaves fell last year,
I am standing underneath to wait for them to sprout new.
I then go to wake up the sleeping stream,
Listening to it sing and running with it together.

After being tired of walking, I lie down in the field.
There is the sun shining brightly overhead.
Who is tickling my cheeks?
It must be the tender grass who comes out nearby.

Written in 1980

The rain

Outside the window,
It has been raining heavily.
But, Mom, please
Do not stop me.
I want to dash into the rain.

I put on a straw hat,
And run into the heavy rain.
I turn into an umbrella,
That flies in the windy rain
To protect people without umbrellas from getting wet in the rain.

When the rain stops,
I fly away once more
Into the dense forest
After being washed by the rain.

Mom, perhaps
You cannot find your daughter.
I know you are worrying about me,
About me getting wet in the rain.

You run into the street,
Asking the wind after the rain,
Asking the rainbow in the sky,
And asking each person passing by:
Can you tell me
where my daughter is?

You come into the forest,
Asking the little bird,
Asking the blooming flowers,
And asking the raindrops
Dripping down from the leaves:
Can you tell me
where my daughter is?

They all answer in the same:
How naughty
The little girl is!
She must play hide-and-seek
Once again with us. We have no idea this time
Where on earth she is hiding.

In the forest after the rain,
The mushrooms are scattering all over the
ground.
What they like the most
Is to play after the rain.
Mom, when you
Are going to pick up
The whitest
And plumpest mushroom,
It suddenly changes
Into your little daughter,
Who is blinking
And looking at you with a smile.

Oh, Mom,

I am back.

Look at me please.

I am still wearing the straw hat,

With colourful raindrops

Staying on.

Written in 1980

A deer

With the shadow of flowers and that of the leaves,
You are made
For a colourful dress.

You stand over there,
Integrating into
The boundless forest.

You also seem to be a running tree,
Holding up your branched antlers
And dashing into the dense forest.

You are talking about the news of spring
With this tree for a while,
And with that tree for another while.

Written in 1980

A song of small tree

Small tree
sways in the spring breeze,
trying to secretly decorate its sprouts,
and all the treetops with the beautiful green.

Small tree,
Sways in the spring breeze,
Dying its pistils,
As well as the buds in the gorgeous red.

It calls
The singing bird,
Saying:
When I grow up,
I can hardly be blown down
By a raging storm.
You will be safe to build a lovely home
Among my strong branches and dense leaves.

Written in 1980

Letters

I have learned to write letters,
With pen and paper,
With hand and heart.
How eagerly I want to write
Piles and piles of letters.

Write to the mother bird for her baby
To ask her to come back to the nest,
As it is almost dusk.

Write to the busy bees for flowers
To inform them to collect honey,
As the flowers are in full bloom.

Write to the boat for the sea
To encourage it to go sailing,
As the sea is calm.

Write to the cloud for another cloud
To express the wishes of turning into a spring drizzle.
Write to the tree for another tree
To show their intention to form an endless forest.

For myself,
I also want to write
Many letters
To remind myself
In connecting with the others
Closely and tightly.

Written in 1980

28

Stars and flowers

I love summer the most.

Flowers are all over the world:

One is here,

And one is there,

Which are more than the stars who are twinkling in the sky.

When it is at night,

Flowers all fall into the deep sleep.

I start to count the stars over my head:

One is here,

And one is there,

Which are on the contrary more than the flowers swaying on

the ground.

Written in 1980

A leaf whistle

With a small and thin leaf,
Wonderful music can be easily played.

Like a bird chirping on a tree,
Melodiously and gently;
Like a stream running under the trees,
Softly and crystally;
Like the breeze whistling in the forest,
Joyfully and nimbly.

The music played by the leaf whistle is
More delightful than the bird,
More affectionate than the stream,
And more active than the breeze.
Such green leaves can be found everywhere.
My lovely hometown is exactly a world full of music.

Written in 1981

31

Memory

I still remember,
One day in my childhood,
I was singing,
Whilst walking across the grass.

Suddenly, in the grass
Flashed a dazzling colour.
I quivered,
Just like something skimming across my back.
Oh dear! I saw a snake.

I escaped as far as I could,
Watching the snake
Wiggling in the grass,
And Swimming through the river.
I seemingly felt a cold wind blowing.
It slowly and quietly
Crawled up an old tree,
Turning into a branch,
And hiding among the leaves.

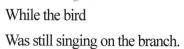

While the bird
Was still singing on the branch.

All in a sudden, the snake
Flew over
To catch the poor bird,
And to unexpectedly pause
The lovely song that the bird had not finished yet.

(What I saw
Was just a few coloured feathers
Falling down like dead leaves...)

In my childhood memory,
There were glittering stars and the glowing moon,
As well as the flowers blooming in the spring.
However, what I
Could never forget
Was the song yet finished by the bird...

Written in 1983

The White Swan

A cloud, floating in the sky,
And falling down in the middle of the lake,
Is a white swan.
Who is he waiting for?

Another cloud, floating in the sky,
And falling down in the middle of the lake,
Is still a white swan.
Who is she looking for?

The two white swans swim side by side,
As close as Mom and Dad.
I wish I could become a little swan,
Following them tightly.

Written in 1985

The black butterfly

Probably due to being used
To the darkness in the forest,
The butterfly always
Dressed in black.

Suddenly, a gust of wind
Blew it out of the forest.
People immediately discovered
Its glorious body shining in the sun.

The world was found by the butterfly.
The butterfly was exposed to the world.

Written in 1986

Transforming

Is that you, the butterfly?

You seem to be a snowflake that will never melt,

Flying in my house.

With your white wings,

You are knocking the window.

Is that you, the butterfly?

Where are you from?

It is now cold December.

We met in spring.

You flew to the fields in summer.

Where did you hide in autumn?

Butterfly, my dear butterfly,

It is now cold December.

In fact,
You are not the one in spring.
Nor the one in summer.
You are the chrysalis
I buried in the flowerpot.
Throughout the whole winter,
You are in my house,
Dreaming of spring.

You wake up early,
And transform afterwards
Into a butterfly.

But, my dear butterfly,
December is very cold.
The icicles hanging upside down outside the window,
Seem to be the sharp teeth.

I ask:

Who will go to the Butterfly Spring in Dali?

Who will go to the Ultima Thule in Hainan?

Who will go to the Coconut grove in Xishuangbanna?

Who will go to Koto island on the other side of Taiwan

Straits?

Please take this butterfly with you.

It's extremely cold here.

It is now December.

Thousands of snowflakes are falling outside the

window.

They are not the dancing butterflies.

I open the window,

Butterfly, my dear butterfly,

Please look outside.

It is a severely cold world.

You abruptly discover,
On such a snowy day,
You have found
So many companions.
You fly out of the window,
Into the vast snowy world.

In order to follow you,
I run into the world of ice and snow.
But I can't find you anymore,
As you have transformed again,
Into a white snowflake.

At the moment, it is the snowy December.
I look up at the white butterflies dancing in the sky...

Written in 1987

You shouldn't just remember

You shouldn't just remember
Milk is poured out
from the bottle,
But should also know,
Milk is milked out
Of the cows—
They come from the prairie,
Which is vast and faraway.

You shouldn't just remember
The apple is taken out
Of Grandma's basket,
But should also know,
The apple is plucked
from the tree—
Apple trees grow on the ground,
The soil of which is dark and fertile,
Mixed in addition with people's sweat.

You shouldn't just remember
You are the child of your parents,
But should also know,
Everyone has their own parents—
In such a big world,
There are millions of people,
Who live together by the same sun.

You should not only remember what others give,
But also know how to reward.

Written in 1987

The Illusion

Outside the school wall,

There is a spacious square,

A street garden,

Boulevards,

The lawn,

flowerbeds,

and birds.

The slender alley is ahead if going further.

Whenever I walk home from school,

I often involuntarily have an illusion:

Can I be the cloud floating over the square?

Can I be the flower blooming in the street garden?

Can I be the tree standing on the boulevard?

Or be a new-planted grass in the lawn,

Or a bird reflected in the dewdrops on the grass,

Or even a white fluffy dandelion,

Keeping flying, flying over the roofs of the school and my home.

Written in 1988

The Acacia Tree

A blooming acacia tree,
Lighted the red candles full of the trees.
Today, a pair of birds were married.
They received many precious gifts.

A touch of fragrance
Wafted out of the acacia tree.
With such a scent,
A leaf whistle was played by a breeze.

The leaves of the acacia tree,
Like the soft feathers,
Swaying gently
In the tender breeze.

Birds coming from far away,
Gifted their gorgeous feathers,
To newlywed birds
To make a comfortable nest.

When the night fell and the stars twinkled,
At the time the newlywed birds were going to sleep,
The leaves of the acacia tree
Then closed their eyelashes...

Written in 1989

The Campus Story

The campus story is a river.

The campus story is a song.

The shadow of time is floating in the river.

The song is about you and me.

The campus story is a poem.

The campus story is a fairy tale.

Smiles and tears are in the poem,

You and I will never grow up in the fairy tale.

The campus story is a gentle morning breeze.

The campus story is a rustling spring rain.

The wind and rain transmit the whispers.

The secret in my heart is also sprouting.

The breeze blows away the singing.

The running water drifts away the falling flowers.

Only the campus story is endless,

While you and I who used to be in the story have already

grown up.

Written in 1990

A moonlit night in the woods

The gentle moonlight
Seems to be the glittering spring water,
Shining on every green leaf,
And dazzling a glorious glimmer.

The leaves stand still,
Dreaming quietly.
They dream of the moonlight turning into,
Crystal
and exquisite dewdrops,
Swaying down in the morning breeze
One by one...
Jingling,
Jingling,
And tinkling.

Written in 1990

Wishing to stand as a tree

Only when you walk into the forest can you
Really understand the birds' chirping.

It is a sound awakened by the morning light.
It is a sound moisten by the dew.
It is a sound soaked in the floral fragrance.

The chirping is about a story between the trees.
The chirping is about the intimacy between the leaves.
The chirping is about a secret among flowers.

Wish to stand as a tree, so as to
Understand the birds' chirping indeed.

Written in 1990

The mountain

Overlook the distant mountain—
The mountain is small,
While I am big.
I am the person appreciating a painting.
The mountain is the painting.

Walk into the remote mountain—
The mountain is huge,
While I am tiny.
The mountain seems to be a green sea.
I am like a bird.

Written in 1991

The Brook

When seeing you running,

I would like to crawl on the ground,

Listening to your story.

Your story is very long,

Which is about:

In the distance,

There is a little girl,

Who will never grow up.

She, like a brook,

Will be happy forever,

And always be delight and bright.

(The brook is running,

Bringing the floral fragrance from the distance.)

Written in 1991

Flying starts right here

On this land
Grow the dense trees,
In which there are birds' nests.
The chicks are nurtured in the nests.

They are getting more and more feathers,
While their singing becomes more and more beautiful.
They are learning how to fly
So that they can fly right up into the clear sky.

Even if the birds can fly high and far,
They will never forget their nests.
The nests belong to the trees, while the trees to the land.
Hence, their lives of flying start right here.

Written in 1992

Listening

It was Mom's singing that taught me how to listen.
She gifted me a pair of real ears.
I've been listening since I was a child,
Listening to the wonderful music of nature.

I listen to the stream running in the valley,
Listen to the birds singing at dawn,
Listen to the whispers under the eaves, and
Listen to the sorrow of the wind chimes hanging on the ancient pagoda.

I also listen to the love words spoken by the bees to flowers,
Listen to the advice given by the autumn wind to the fallen leaves.
These warm and melodious songs,
Will be cherished in my heart forever.

Written in 1992

The boat is floating away

When travelling through the arch of the ancient
bridge,
It seems to say goodbye to a small town.
The water world outside the town is broad, and
Beautiful sceneries are everywhere—

After passing a cast of reeds,
The lotuses are encountered, which are red and
blooming in full.
The boat is swaying on the clear water,
An osprey standing on the fore.

The old stone bridge is still standing there,
Seeing off the boat that is floating away.
The bridge arch is reflected in the water,
Like the reflection of a full moon.

Written in 1993

Woods in the Rain

Woods in the rain are a fairy tale paradise.
When you walk in, you will become an elf.
Every tree will give you many things nice.
You will find novel stuff all by yourself.

The crystal raindrops roll from side to side on the leaves.
A spider spins silk very hard to make you a necklace.
Carpets made of fallen flowers are soft, fragrance interweaves.
Frogs keep drumming and dancing, performance for you never
endless.

The birds too, are willing to sing in the rain.
The listener squirrels are shaking their furry tails.
The berries taste sour and sweet after nourished by the rain,
Which are taken home secretly on the hedgehogs' quills.

Even those little raindrops are able to perform magic tricks.
They instantly turn into mushrooms after falling on the bricks.

Written in 1994

There is actually no wind blowing

There is actually no wind blowing,

But little flowers still fall from the branches,

Without even saying a goodbye.

Silence is an affectionate song.

Just for another life,

Just for another happiness,

Just for the fruits after blossoms falling,

Little flowers still fall from the branches.

Written in 1994

Pomegranate blossoms are again as red as fire

Pomegranate blossoms are again as red as fire,

Blazing on the branches.

The memory is also lit up.

Summer anew crawls up the treetops.

Wind makes the blossoms

Even more enchanting.

Burning is life.

Burning is joy.

Written in 1994

A green leaf is keeping silent.

The whole forest is having a shower in the drizzle,
Each single leaf is clapping with the little wet hands.
The forest is in the glittering green clothes with whistle,
Every branch is swaying in the rain and gradually extends.

All but one green leaf doesn't talk and keep silent.
It resists the wind and rain by curling itself up.
With the pitter patter of rain in a world this quiet,
It becomes a small tent that can be set up.

Can you please guess who indeed lives in the tent?
It turns out to be a small seven-star beetle,
Appreciating the beauty of rain in the forest that is blent,
And sleeping with the rain, the same as other people.

The sound of rain at the night dripped into the dream.
I find myself become a little beetle in my own dream.

Written in 1994

The breeze has no intention

Just coming
Gently and quietly,
It can't be seen,
Nor be touched.

The peach blossoms have fallen on the ground,
While the new grown grass is a bit taller.
Even the long-lost grey magpie
Has flown into the woods.

Inadvertently, arrives
The drizzle, walking
Briskly
across the small stone bridge.

I stand in the rain,
Feeling the breeze.

Written in 1995

Cicadas

Cicadas in the sunset
Are chirping even louder.

The sound of cicadas makes the path in the forest
Fade into the twilight.

Together, we
Quickly go down the mountain.

If getting lost,
Who are you going to ask?

Cicadas chirp loudly,
But they are actually deaf.

Written in 1995

Muttering

When the autumn wind blows,

The sunset is extremely cold.

After the Mid-Autumn Festival,

The taste of fruits seems to be as rich as remembered.

Under the eaves, there is

No muttering of the past heard any more.

When did the swallow leave?

When will it come back?

Since then, on the night with moonlight glowing,

I often fall asleep with the wind whistling.

I can hear myself muttering to the swallow

Till dawn.

Written in 1995

A horseshoe

The herdsman was out of sight on the grassland,

With the tramp of hoofs behind.

Like planting the seeds of life,

He has left his horseshoe.

In every footprint,

There was a sad sense of nostalgia.

On that horseshoe,

Each rust spot contained a story of time.

I hung it on the wall,

Like dropping the anchor in the sea.

Wish the unknown traveller

Has arrived home safely.

Written in 1995

84

Elm tree seeds

Falling in the wind
Are clusters of elm tree seeds.

That elm tree is very, very old,
Planted by Grandfather's grandfather.

At their age, it was really gloomy and cold,
As well as often raining.

The elm tree seeds in such rainy weather
Gradually turned into a rusty green.

Written in 1995

On the days with umbrella

On the days with umbrella,
Another piece of sky is lifted.
There is a reminder of rain over head,
Remote but gentle.

On the days with umbrella,
Another stretch of land is paved.
The grass under the feet raises its head,
Goggling with its bright eyes.

On the days with umbrella,
Every drop of rain is a melody.
I become a little note,
Melting into the world of rain.

Written in 1995

Reading about the shadow of mine

When I was young, I could not read.
I enjoyed sitting there,
Reading about the shadow of mine,
Like reading a book of fairy tales.

I always found a black bear,
Or a few dark bunnies,
Who sat and lay down on my feet,
And kept speaking to me.

Until the sun set
When the shadow disappeared,
I was completely left alone.

I knew, tomorrow,
The shadow would come again,
And there would be new stories...

Written in 1995

Bird's Nest

The bird's nest is
Another kind of scenery of a tree.
The bird's nest is
Another life of the tree.

The tree without a nest
Lives a lonely and desolate life,
Leaves talking to leaves,
Roots and soil listening.

The tree with a nest
Is like a tree with a blooming flower.
In the nest,
The sun rises at dawn,
The moon raises up at night,
Nestlings keep talking to the stars.

The nest makes the silent tree happy.
The nest makes the life of the tree lively.

Written in 1997

Composing music
for March

With the gurgling sound of the running stream,
With the fragrance of the sprouting branches,
With the whispers of the flying swallow,
Compose music for March.

With the soft grass standing by the river,
With the dove whistle lingering in the clear sky,
With the quiet and silent drizzle,
Compose music for March.

The song of March is dancing.

The song of March is flashing.

The song of March is frolicking.

On the treetops,

In the bird's nest,

Among the clouds,

Wafts

The song of March.

When dripping on the wings of a butterfly,

When dripping in the heart of the fragrant flowers,

And when dripping into the twinkling eyes,

Spring is even more beautiful, and its beauty is—

In the Song of March.

Written in 1998

The Bird's Chirping
Cleanses the Morning

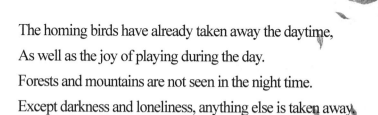

The homing birds have already taken away the daytime,
As well as the joy of playing during the day.
Forests and mountains are not seen in the night time.
Except darkness and loneliness, anything else is taken away.

The bird's chirping is the first sound heard at dawn.
It thoroughly cleanses the misty fog in the morning.
The dewdrops open their bright eyes on the lawn.
With gorgeous clothes, the forest is adorning.

The morning cleansed by the bird's chirping is gorgeous,
As brilliant as the flowers with dewdrops on.
The morning cleansed by the bird's chirping is luscious,
As delicious as the sweet and juicy melon.

Greet a new day in the bird's chirping.
Even in the songs, brilliant light is shining.

Written in 1998

There Are Also Bright Colours in Deep Autumn

There are also bright colours in deep autumn.

The last persimmon is still hanging on the branch,
In the dazzling orange red.
Three bullfinches are flying over,
Blinking their eyes timidly.

Looking at the trembling branches,
The bullfinches to and fro.
After gradually approaching to the persimmon,
They start to share the taste of autumn.

I see Grandpa standing in front of the window,
Looking at the three bullfinches,
And an orange-red persimmon.
His white beard is shaking.

There are also bright colours in deep autumn.

Written in 2000

Fish by candlelight

Time puts on a black shirt.
Here comes the night.

Heart is floating freely,
Like invisible fish.

Lighting up a red candle,
I see my own shadow cast on the wall.
(Is that me?)

Facing the fish by candlelight,
As a flower in the water,
I see my heart blooming.

Written in 2000

The evening breeze is hiding in the flowers

The evening breeze is hiding in the flowers,

No whistles,

Nor noises,

Like falling asleep, it is completely quiet.

In fact, it is whispering to the flowers:

I would like to have a house,

I would like to have a home,

I would like to have a dad and a mom.

The green leave and red flower are answering together:

The green leave will be your dad,

The red flower will be your mom,

This cluster of flowers will be your home.

Written in 2000

I Met a White Bird
on a Rainy Day

The drizzle painted the leaves green and the flowers red.

Everything in the world was listening to the tranquillity.

A white bird seemed to be a beam of light,

Landing gorgeously onto the slate road with ability.

The twittering of it was seemingly a beautiful song,

Listening to which you would feel easy and free.

The white bird was briskly hopping along.

Its joy on the road was the same as flying.

I was coming over and met with the white bird.

Both of us stopped moving at the same time.

After staring for a minute at the little bird,

We talked and returned to silence after some time.

We had no fear of each other but love instead.

The short talk was like the one for our entire life.

Written in 2001

Black Ant

Little black ant,
Why do you climb to the tree?
You are not a bird.
There is no home in the tree.

Black ant clings to the big tree,
Without even a movement.
Quietly and carefully,
It is listening to the heartbeat of the tree.

One is a big tree,
One is a little ant;
One is very tall,
One is too small.

The dearest voice ever heard
Must be the powerful heartbeat.

Written in 2003

The Fallen Tree

Even if the tree falls down,
It is till alive;
For listening to the bird singing,
it grows countless ears.

The tree and the bird
used to live together.
The tree once stood,
Waiting for the bird
To fly up
And to land down.

Written in 2003

White Clouds

White clouds
Are floating
Slowly and gently.

Floating over the treetops,
Floating over the peaks,
It has gone without a trace to find.

Until seeing a child sketching,
(Who is painting a forest,
A stream,
As well as the clear sky.)
White clouds
Finally stop floating and drift into the child's painting.

Written in 2004

The Wind Passes Through My Fingers

The wind passes through my fingers.
I have felt the wind.
I clench my palm.

There is flower fragrance in the wind.
There is bird twittering in the wind.
There is singing in the wind.

I open my palm.
The wind is a free elf,
Passing through my fingers.

Written in 2004

Take me home

In the morning glow, the scenery of the
alley was
An unfolded scroll painting.
I saw Mom walking home
With a vegetable basket in her hand.

There were still dewdrops on the leaves,
And a butterfly flying around her.
A familiar fragrance was wafting out
From the watery leaves.

On Mom's forehead,
Droplets of sweat were welling up.
I ran over
Into her arms.

Memories of never growing up,
Paintings that would never fade,
Could always hear those soft words:
Mom, take me home...

Written in 2004

A cat leads the night to walk

A cat is proudly leading the night to walk.

The night gets darker while the cat whiter.

Who opens the mystic curtain and stop people's talk?

Stars dashing onto the stage make the world brighter.

To listen to the song that had lost for ages,

All the old trees are slowly gathering together.

The cat's whiteness lights up the night and nearby faces.

How many friends will reunite on tonight's nice weather?

The bird dives into the lake to swim at the bottom.

The fish leaped into the night sky to freely fly.

The white cat and the dark night exchange their welcome.

The evening breeze gently blows flower fragrance into the sky.

What they are embracing is each other's soul.

Before you know, the night is dark as coal.

Written in 2007

You can see me even
if you close your eyes

At the moment, the breeze no longer blows.

At the moment, the fireflies stop flying.

The remote and close lights no longer flicker.

The flowers on the fields have all fallen asleep.

I walk through your dreams,

Where you can see me even if you close your eyes.

I will decorate the flowers with dew.

I will turn the leaves into emeralds.

I will make the birds' feathers even more plump,

So that we can fly together towards the dawn.

I will send you a song in your dreams,
Where you can see me even if you close your eyes.

I would like to have a date with stars.
I would like to comfort the loneliness.
I would like to sing a lullaby to a baby.
I would like to take glory to the dreams.

Please remember my promise in your dreams,
Where you can see me even if you close your eyes.

Facing the distant mountains and the nearby lakes,
Please allow my soul to embrace you to sleep.
When we meet again in the morning glow,
I really want you to guess who I am.

Anyone who has met me in the dreams
Can see me even if he closes his eyes.

Written in 2008

I want to be smaller

I want to be smaller,

So that I can enter the drift bottle,

Wandering in the crowds of people.

I don't know who I will meet.

But whoever he is,

I am full of curiosity.

I am looking forward to

The unexpected encounters,

As we are all eager to be cared for.

I extremely hope to see you,

A little girl picking up the shells,

Who walks on the beach with her bare feet.

I will get out of the bottle,

And hold your hands

To go along the beach without wearing the shoes…

Written in 2008

I am a
butterfly

I am a butterfly.
In late autumn,
Please put me in
A thick book of epics.

Fly over five thousand years.
Wander in the lines.
Feel the tranquillity of a moonlit night.
Read about neighs of war horses.

Listen to the morning bell and evening
drum.
Watch the river surging.
The drizzle
Gently strokes my wings.

If someone opens the book,
I will be a resurrected butterfly,
Flying onto the branch,
And turning into a new sprout.

Written in 2013

122

A thinking stone

I unexpectedly want to become
A thinking stone,
Sitting still,
And never moving.

(When turning to a stone, I will not be diagnosed
To suffer "hyperactivity disorder".)

With green shade over the head,

Blooming flowers standing around,

And little birds on the shoulder,

I can greatly enjoy their beautiful chirping.

Greet to the morning glow,

And watch the stars at night.

When turning to a thinking stone,

I lead to a completely full and interesting life.

As a quiet and silent person,

I am thinking about serious matters.

Indeed, I understand people become smart

After learning how to think.

Just imagine, it is getting darker,

And evening breeze keeps blowing,

When suddenly recalling the warm house that

Mom is in,

I will probably start to walk home slowly and

quietly...

Written in 1999

Taking a stone back home

King's Peak, Lion Peak, Yu'nv Peak,
Lingxiao Peak, Shengri Peak, Tianyou Peak...

We believed that each peak
Was an enormous stone.
When clambering from this side of the peak to that side,
We were like ants, climbing on the rock.

Reaching King's Peak: the first dangerous one,
We listened to the legend of the King Yu'nv.
Climbing up to the shoulders of Yu'nv Peak,
We whispered to her
And told her our secrets.
Arriving at Tianyou Peak, we saw the clouds changing.
I was wondering whether the mountain was floating or I was...

Next to the grass, under the wildflowers,

Or on the bank of Jiuqu Stream,

We picked up any stone,

And left it on the palm.

When staring at the stone,

We would have new discovery:

The water in Jiuqu Stream and all the thirty-

six Peaks

Would revolve each stone before moving on.

Taking a stone back home,

I could fiddle with it for my entire life.

Written in 2013

A common rock

Even if you are a common rock,
When I hold you in my arms,
You will be a mountain.

With lots of rocks,
I build up my home,
Where I am instead in the arms of the rocks.

If I am left in the mountains,
I wish to become a rock,
Staying close to the earth.

If anyone dares to chop me with a sharp axe,
I will burst out sparks,
As well as show a burning sign.

Written in 2013

Saying something more
(Postscript)

After compiling this book of poems, I have been through the lines written by myself. I have a feeling that I have crossed my childhood, youth, middle age, and reached the old age. As accompanied by poetry for so many years, I believe the whole period is warm. Even if it was sometimes tranquil outside, there would be the singing inside.

I often think about this question: Why do I write poems for children, which lasts for sixty years?

The strength of persistence lies in my mind. There are many children living inside me, and the most important and closest one is myself. It is the acquaintance, communication, friendship, happiness and sorrow, memories and thoughts between me and many children that form the strength of such persistence.

The children's world is not small. Their minds are broader and more complicated, quite a lot of which is not known to the adults. We may be happy but was paid no attention. We may feel sad but was overlooked.

When we make stories for ourselves and are exhilarated with what we have done, who will come and listen to us carefully?

Accordingly, as a child, my body flies in space, and my soul floats in fantasy.

We learn to speak to nature, and subsequently enter poetry. Poems make what we see extremely beautiful and what we feel deep warm. I am accompanied by both fantasy and poetry.

Childhood is an asset and also the source of creation.

People who learn to remember their childhood, cherish their childhood, appreciate their childhood, and understand their childhood will have a richer life or even a poetic life.

The poems selected for this collection are dreams of childhood, stories of childhood, and fantasies of childhood. The scenes in the poems are memories of childhood.

Due to loving the project of this set of poems, appreciating the binding design, and lauding the meticulous work done by the publisher and their editors, I would like to say something more to show my sincere gratitude.

JIN Bo

9th April 2017